Eileen,

Let familiarity breed delight!

Merry Christmas 2004.

Sandy

best loved poems

best loved poems

This edition published in 2003 and reprinted in 2004 by

Advanced Marketing (UK) Ltd, Bicester, Oxfordshire

Designed by seagulls

Printed in Thailand by Imago

ISBN 1903938317

Now Sleeps the Crimson Petal

Now sleeps the crimson petal, now the white;
Nor waves the cypress in the palace walk;
Nor winks the gold fin in the porphyry font:
The fire-fly wakens: waken thou with me.

Now droops the milkwhite peacock like a ghost,
And like a ghost she glimmers on to me.

Now lies the Earth all Danaë to the stars,
And all thy heart lies open unto me.

Now slides the silent meteor on, and leaves
A shining furrow, as thy thoughts in me.

Now folds the lily all her sweetness up,
And slips into the bosom of the lake:
So fold thyself, my dearest, thou, and slip
Into my bosom and be lost in me.

ALFRED, LORD TENNYSON

The Lake Isle of Innisfree

I will arise and go now, and go to Innisfree,
And a small cabin build there, of clay and wattles made:
Nine bean-rows will I have there, a hive for the honey-bee,
And live alone in the bee-loud glade.

And I shall have some peace there, for peace comes dropping slow,
Dropping from the veils of the morning to where the cricket sings;
There midnight's all a glimmer, and noon a purple glow,
And evening full of the linnet's wings.

I will arise and go now, for always night and day
I hear lake water lapping with low sounds by the shore;
While I stand on the roadway, or on the pavements grey,
I hear it in the deep heart's core.

WILLIAM BUTLER YEATS

lake water
lapping with low
sounds by the shore...

now at the
last gasp
of love's
latest breath...

'Since there's no help,
come let us kiss and part'

Since there's no help, come let us kiss and part.
Nay, I have done; you get no more of me,
And I am glad, yea, glad with all my heart,
That thus so cleanly I myself can free;
Shake hands for ever, cancel all our vows,
And when we meet at any time again,

Be it not seen in either of our brows
   That we one jot of former love retain.
Now at the last gasp of Love's latest breath,
   When, his pulse failing, Passion speechless lies,
When Faith is kneeling by his bed of death,
   And Innocence is closing up his eyes,
      Now if thou wouldst, when all have given him over,
      From death to life thou mightst him yet recover

the beauty of the morning; silent, bare...

Upon Westminster Bridge
Sept. 3, 1802

Earth has not anything to show more fair:

    Dull would he be of soul who could pass by

    A sight so touching in its majesty:

This City now doth, like a garment, wear

The beauty of the morning; silent, bare,

    Ships, towers, domes, theatres, and temples lie

    Open unto the fields, and to the sky;

All bright and glittering in the smokeless air.

Never did sun more beautifully steep

    In his first splendour, valley, rock, or hill;

Ne'er saw I, never felt, a calm so deep!

    The river glideth at his own sweet will:

Dear God! the very houses seem asleep;

    And all that mighty heart is lying still!

WILLIAM WORDSWORTH

Sonnet XVIII

'Shall I compare thee to a summer's day?'

Shall I compare thee to a summer's day?
  Thou art more lovely and more temperate:
Rough winds do shake the darling buds of May,
  And summer's lease hath all too short a date:
Sometime too hot the eye of heaven shines,
  And often is his gold complexion dimmed;
And every fair from fair sometime declines,
  By chance, or nature's changing course untrimmed;
But thy eternal summer shall not fade,
  Nor lose possession of that fair thou owest,
Nor shall Death brag thou wanderest in his shade,
  When in eternal lines to time thou growest;
    So long as men can breathe, or eyes can see,
    So long lives this, and this gives life to thee.

WILLIAM SHAKESPEARE

so long lives this,
and this gives life to thee

To Celia

Drink to me only with thine eyes,
    And I will pledge with mine;
Or leave a kiss but in the cup
    And I'll not look for wine.
The thirst that from the soul doth rise
    Doth ask a drink divine;
But might I of Jove's nectar sup,

I sent thee late a rosy wreath,
    Not so much honouring thee
As giving it a hope that there
    It could not withered be;
But thou thereon didst only breathe,
    And sent'st it back to me;
Since when it grows, and smells, I swear,

Sonnet X
'Death, be not proud'

Death, be not proud, though some have callèd thee
   Mighty and dreadful, for thou art not so;
   For those whom thou think'st thou dost overthrow
Die not, poor Death, nor yet canst thou kill me.
From rest and sleep, which but thy pictures be,
   Much pleasure – then, from thee much more must flow;
   And soonest our best men with thee do go,
Rest of their bones and soul's delivery.
Thou'rt slave to fate, chance, kings and desperate men,
   And dost with poison, war, and sickness dwell;
   And poppy or charms can make us sleep as well,
And better than thy stroke. Why swell'st thou then?
   One short sleep past, we wake eternally,
   And death shall be no more. Death, thou shalt die.

JOHN DONNE

one short sleep past, we wake eternally...

from Kubla Khan

In Xanadu did Kubla Khan
   A stately pleasure-dome decree:
Where Alph, the sacred river, ran
Through caverns measureless to man
   Down to a sunless sea.
So twice five miles of fertile ground
With walls and towers were girdled round:
And there were gardens bright with sinuous rills
Where blossomed many an incense-bearing tree;
And here were forests ancient as the hills,
Enfolding sunny spots of greenery.

But O, that deep romantic chasm which slanted
Down the green hill athwart a cedarn cover!
A savage place! as holy and enchanted
As e'er beneath a waning moon was haunted
By woman wailing for her demon-lover!

through wood
and dale the
sacred river ran...

And from this chasm, with ceaseless turmoil seething,

As if this earth in fast thick pants were breathing,

A mighty fountain momently was forced;

Amid whose swift half-intermitted burst

Huge fragments vaulted like rebounding hail,

Or chaffy grain beneath the thresher's flail:

And 'mid these dancing rocks at once and ever

It flung up momently the sacred river.

Five miles meandering with a mazy motion

Through wood and dale the sacred river ran,

Then reached the caverns measureless to man,

And sank in tumult to a lifeless ocean:

And 'mid this tumult Kubla heard from far

Ancestral voices prophesying war!

SAMUEL TAYLOR COLERIDGE

that looks
on **tempests**
and is
never shaken...

Sonnet CXVI
'Let me not to the marriage of true minds'

Let me not to the marriage of true minds

    Admit impediments. Love is not love

Which alters when it alteration finds,

    Or bends with the remover to remove.

O, no! it is an ever-fixèd mark,

    That looks on tempests and is never shaken;

It is the star to every wandering bark,

    Whose worth's unknown, although his height be taken.

Love's not Time's fool, though rosy lips and cheeks

    Within his bending sickle's compass come;

Love alters not with his brief hours and weeks,

    But bears it out even to the edge of doom.

      If this be error, and upon me proved,

      I never writ, nor no man ever loved.

WILLIAM SHAKESPEARE

Adlestrop

Yes. I remember Adlestrop –
The name, because one afternoon
Of heat the express-train drew up there
Unwontedly. It was late June.

The steam hissed. Someone cleared
  his throat.
No one left and no one came
On the bare platform. What I saw
Was Adlestrop – only the name

And willows, willow-herb, and grass,
And meadowsweet, and haycocks dry,
No whit less still and lonely fair
Than the high cloudlets in the sky.

And for that minute a blackbird sang
Close by, and round him, mistier,
Farther and farther, all the birds
Of Oxfordshire and Gloucestershire.

EDWARD THOMAS

the express-train
drew up there...

of beechen green,
and shadows
numberless...

from Ode to a Nightingale

I

My heart aches, and a drowsy numbness pains
   My sense, as though of hemlock I had drunk,
Or emptied some dull opiate to the drains
   One minute past, and Lethe-wards had sunk:
'Tis not through envy of thy happy lot,
   But being too happy in thy happiness,
      That thou, light-wingèd Dryad of the trees,
         In some melodious plot
   Of beechen green, and shadows numberless,
      Singest of summer in full-throated ease.

II

O for a draught of vintage! that hath been
   Cooled a long age in the deep-delvèd earth,
Tasting of Flora and the country-green,
   Dance, and Provençal song, and sunburnt mirth!
O for a beaker full of the warm South!
   Full of the true, the blushful Hippocrene,
      With beaded bubbles winking at the brim,
         And purple-stainèd mouth;
   That I might drink, and leave the world unseen,
      And with thee fade away into the forest dim:

JOHN KEATS

Sonnet XXX
'When to the sessions
of sweet silent thought'

When to the sessions of sweet silent thought
    I summon up remembrance of things past,
I sigh the lack of many a thing I sought,
    And with old woes new wail my dear time's waste:
Then can I drown an eye, unused to flow,
    For precious friends hid in death's dateless night,
And weep afresh love's long since cancelled woe,
    And moan the expense of many a vanished sight:
Then can I grieve at grievances foregone,
    And heavily from woe to woe tell o'er
The sad account of fore-bemoanèd moan,
    Which I new pay as if not paid before.
      But if the while I think on thee, dear friend,
      All losses are restored, and sorrows end.

WILLIAM SHAKESPEARE

moan the expense
of many a
vanished sight...

near them,
on the sand half-sunk, a
shattered visage lies...

OZYMANDIAS

I met a traveller from an antique land
Who said: Two vast and trunkless legs of stone
Stand in the desert . . . Near them, on the sand,
Half-sunk, a shattered visage lies, whose frown,
And wrinkled lip, and sneer of cold command,
Tell that its sculptor well those passions read
Which yet survive, stamped on these lifeless things,
The hand that mocked them, and the heart that fed:
And on the pedestal these words appear:
'My name is Ozymandias, king of kings:
Look on my works, ye Mighty, and despair!'
Nothing beside remains. Round the decay
Of that colossal wreck, boundless and bare
The lone and level sands stretch far away.

PERCY BYSSHE SHELLEY

Crossing the Bar

Sunset and evening star,
    And one clear call for me!
And may there be no moaning of the bar,
    When I put out to sea,

But such a tide as moving seems asleep,
    Too full for sound and foam,
When that which drew from out the boundless deep
    Turns again home.

Twilight and evening bell,
    And after that the dark!
And may there be no sadness of farewell,
    When I embark;

For though from out our bourne of Time and Place
    The flood may bear me far,
I hope to see my Pilot face to face
    When I have crost the bar.

ALFRED, LORD TENNYSON

such a tide as moving seems asleep...

The Windhover
To Christ our Lord

I caught this morning morning's minion, king-
    dom of daylight's dauphin, dapple-dawn-drawn Falcon, in his riding
    Of the rolling level underneath him steady air, and striding
High there, how he rung upon the rein of a wimpling wing
In his ecstasy! then off, off forth on swing,
    As a skate's heel sweeps smooth on a bow-bend: the hurl and gliding
    Rebuffed the big wind. My heart in hiding
Stirred for a bird, – the achieve of, the mastery of the thing!

Brute beauty and valour and act, oh, air, pride, plume, here
    Buckle! AND the fire that breaks from thee then, a billion
Times told lovelier, more dangerous, O my chevalier!

    No wonder of it: shéer plód makes plough down sillion
Shine, and blue-bleak embers, ah my dear,
    Fall, gall themselves, and gash gold-vermilion.

GERARD MANLEY HOPKINS

of daylight's
dauphin, dapple-dawn-drawn
falcon...

from An Essay on Man

Know then thyself, presume not God to scan;

The proper study of mankind is Man.

Placed on this isthmus of a middle state,

A being darkly wise and rudely great:

With too much knowledge for the Sceptic side,

With too much weakness for the Stoic's pride,

He hangs between; in doubt to act or rest,

In doubt to deem himself a God or Beast,

In doubt his mind or body to prefer;

Born but to die, and reasoning but to err;

Alike in ignorance, his reason such

Whether he thinks too little or too much:

Chaos of thought and passion, all confused;

Still by himself abused, or disabused;

Created half to rise and half to fall;

Great lord of all things, yet a prey to all;

Sole judge of truth, in endless error hurled:

The glory, jest, and riddle of the world!

ALEXANDER POPE

created half
to rise and
half to fall...

a vestige of the thoughts that once i had...

Remember

Remember me when I am gone away,
  Gone far away into the silent land;
  When you can no more hold me by the hand,
Nor I half turn to go yet turning stay.
Remember me when no more day by day
  You tell me of our future that you planned:
  Only remember me; you understand
It will be late to counsel then or pray.
Yet if you should forget me for a while
  And afterwards remember, do not grieve:
  For if the darkness and corruption leave
  A vestige of the thoughts that once I had,
Better by far you should forget and smile
Than that you should remember and be sad

from The Old Vicarage, Grantchester

Ah God! to see the branches stir
Across the moon at Grantchester!
To smell the thrilling-sweet and rotten
Unforgettable, unforgotten
River-smell, and hear the breeze
Sobbing in the little trees.
Say, do the elm-clumps greatly stand
Still guardians of that holy land?
The chestnuts shade, in reverend dream,
The yet unacademic stream?
Is dawn a secret shy and cold
Anadyomene, silver-gold?
And sunset still a golden sea
From Haslingfield to Madingley?
And after, ere the night is born,
Do hares come out about the corn?
Oh, is the water sweet and cool,
Gentle and brown, above the pool?
And laughs the immortal river still
Under the mill, under the mill?
Say, is there Beauty yet to find?
And Certainty? and Quiet kind?
Deep meadows yet, for to forget
The lies, and truths, and pain? . . . oh! yet
Stands the Church clock at ten to three?
And is there honey still for tea?

RUPERT BROOKE

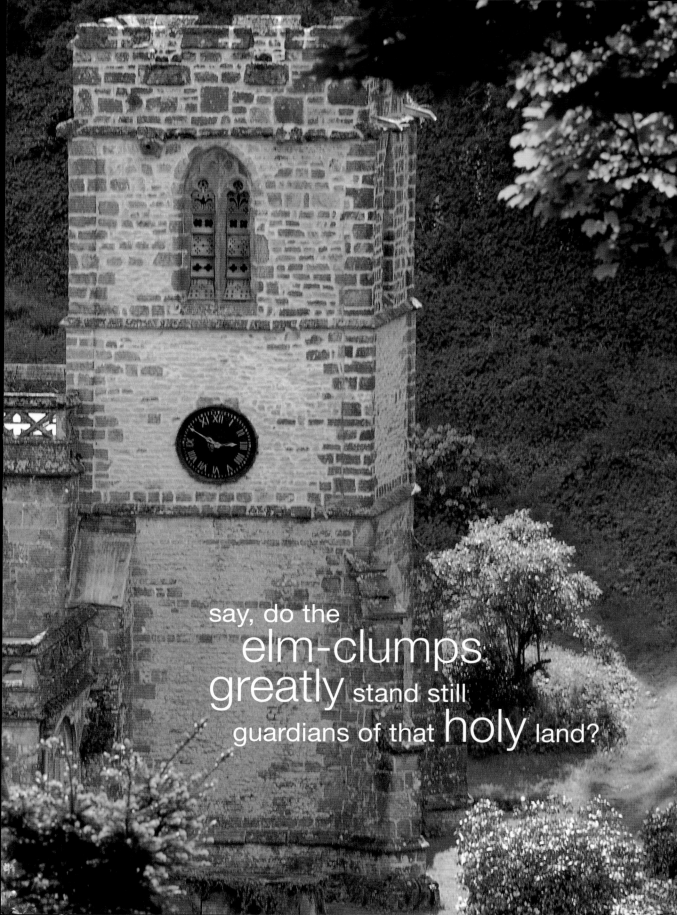

say, do the
elm-clumps
greatly stand still
guardians of that **holy** land?

She Walks in Beauty

She walks in beauty, like the night
    Of cloudless climes and starry skies;
And all that's best of dark and bright
    Meet in her aspect and her eyes:
Thus mellowed to that tender light
    Which heaven to gaudy day denies.

One shade the more, one ray the less,
    Had half impaired the nameless grace
Which waves in every raven tress,
    Or softly lightens o'er her face;
Where thoughts serenely sweet express
    How pure, how dear their dwelling-place.

And on that cheek, and o'er that brow,
    So soft, so calm, yet eloquent,
The smiles that win, the tints that glow,
    But tell of days in goodness spent,
A mind at peace with all below,
    A heart whose love is innocent.

LORD BYRON

thus **mellowed**
to that
tender light...

my love is like a red, red rose that's newly sprung in june...

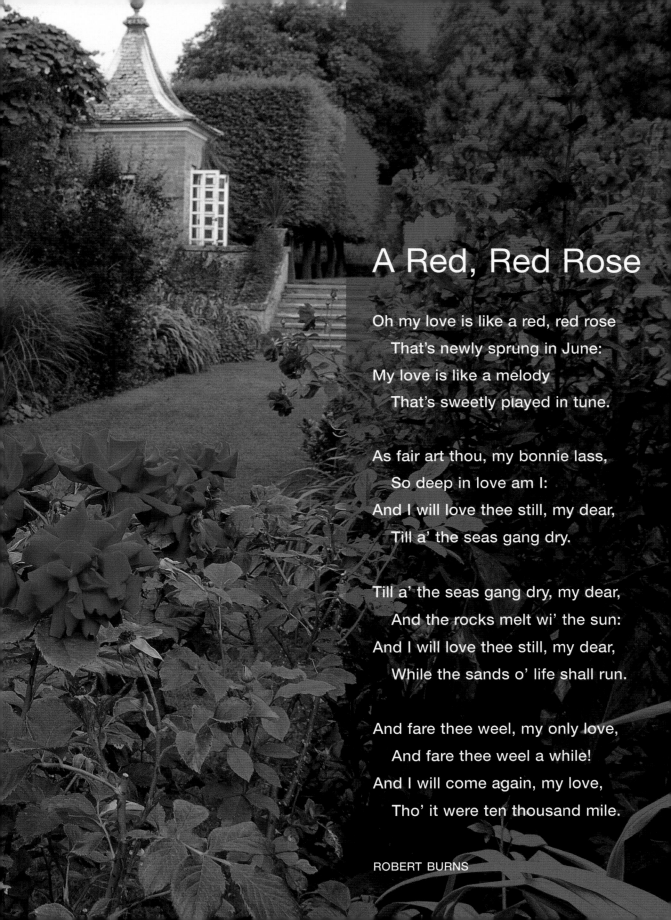

A Red, Red Rose

Oh my love is like a red, red rose
   That's newly sprung in June:
My love is like a melody
   That's sweetly played in tune.

As fair art thou, my bonnie lass,
   So deep in love am I:
And I will love thee still, my dear,
   Till a' the seas gang dry.

Till a' the seas gang dry, my dear,
   And the rocks melt wi' the sun:
And I will love thee still, my dear,
   While the sands o' life shall run.

And fare thee weel, my only love,
   And fare thee weel a while!
And I will come again, my love,
   Tho' it were ten thousand mile.

ROBERT BURNS

Daffodils

I wandered lonely as a cloud
   That floats on high o'er vales and hills,
When all at once I saw a crowd,
   A host, of golden daffodils;
Beside the lake, beneath the trees,
Fluttering and dancing in the breeze.

Continuous as the stars that shine
   And twinkle on the Milky Way,
They stretched in never-ending line
   Along the margin of a bay:
Ten thousand saw I at a glance,
Tossing their heads in sprightly dance.

a host, of golden daffodils; beside the lake, beneath the trees...

The waves beside them danced, but they
  Out-did the sparkling waves in glee:
A poet could not but be gay,
  In such a jocund company:
I gazed – and gazed – but little thought
What wealth the show to me had brought:

For oft, when on my couch I lie
  In vacant or in pensive mood,
They flash upon that inward eye
  Which is the bliss of solitude;
And then my heart with pleasure fills,
And dances with the daffodils.

WILLIAM WORDSWORTH

So, We'll Go No More A-Roving

So, we'll go no more a-roving
   So late into the night,
Though the heart be still as loving,
   And the moon be still as bright.

For the sword outwears its sheath,
   And the soul wears out the breast,
And the heart must pause to breathe,
   And love itself have rest.

Though the night was made for loving,
   And the day returns too soon,
Yet we'll go no more a-roving
   By the light of the moon.

LORD BYRON

the night was made for loving, and the day returns too soon...

from Elegy Written in a Country Churchyard

The curfew tolls the knell of parting day,
The lowing herd wind slowly o'er the lea,
The ploughman homeward plods his weary way,
And leaves the world to darkness and to me.

Now fades the glimmering landscape on the sight,
And all the air a solemn stillness holds,
Save where the beetle wheels his droning flight,
And drowsy tinklings lull the distant folds;

Save that from yonder ivy-mantled tower
The moping owl does to the moon complain
Of such as, wandering near her secret bower,
Molest her ancient solitary reign.

Beneath those rugged elms, that yew-tree's shade,
Where heaves the turf in many a mouldering heap,
Each in his narrow cell for ever laid,
The rude forefathers of the hamlet sleep.

THOMAS GRAY

now fades the
**glimmering
landscape**
on the sight...

Silver

Slowly, silently, now the moon
Walks the night in her silver shoon;
This way, and that, she peers, and sees
Silver fruit upon silver trees;
One by one the casements catch
Her beams beneath the silvery thatch;
Couched in his kennel, like a log,
With paws of silver sleeps the dog;
From their shadowy cote the white breasts peep
Of doves in a silver-feathered sleep;
A harvest mouse goes scampering by,
With silver claws and silver eye;
And moveless fish in the water gleam,
By silver reeds in a silver stream.

WALTER DE LA MARE

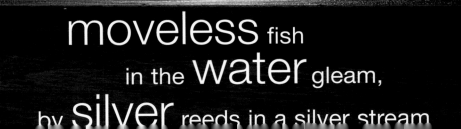

moveless fish
in the water gleam,
by silver reeds in a silver stream

Home Thoughts from Abroad

Oh, to be in England
Now that April's there,
And whoever wakes in England
Sees, some morning, unaware,
That the lowest boughs and the brushwood sheaf
Round the elm-tree bole are in tiny leaf,
While the chaffinch sings on the orchard bough
In England – now!

And after April, when May follows,
And the whitethroat builds, and all the swallows!
Hark, where my blossomed pear-tree in the hedge
Leans to the field and scatters on the clover
Blossoms and dewdrops – at the bent spray's edge –
That's the wise thrush; he sings each song twice over,
Lest you should think he never could recapture
The first fine careless rapture!
And though the fields look rough with hoary dew
All will be gay when noontide wakes anew
The buttercups, the little children's dower
– Far brighter than this gaudy melon-flower!

ROBERT BROWNING

the chaffinch sings
on the orchard bough...

a grey mist on the sea's face and a grey dawn breaking...

Sea-fever

I must go down to the seas again, to the lonely sea and the sky,

And all I ask is a tall ship and a star to steer her by,

And the wheel's kick and the wind's song and the white sail's shaking,

And a grey mist on the sea's face and a grey dawn breaking.

I must go down to the seas again, for the call of the running tide

Is a wild call and a clear call that may not be denied;

And all I ask is a windy day with the white clouds flying,

And the flung spray and the blown spume, and the sea-gulls crying.

I must go down to the seas again, to the vagrant gypsy life,

To the gull's way and the whale's way where the wind's like a whetted knife;

And all I ask is a merry yarn from a laughing fellow-rover,

And quiet sleep and a sweet dream when the long trick's over.

JOHN MASEFIELD

The Soldier

If I should die, think only this of me:
    That there's some corner of a foreign field
That is for ever England. There shall be
    In that rich earth a richer dust concealed;
A dust whom England bore, shaped, made aware,
    Gave, once, her flowers to love, her ways to roam,
A body of England's, breathing English air,
    Washed by the rivers, blest by suns of home.

And think, this heart, all evil shed away,
    A pulse in the eternal mind, no less
        Gives somewhere back the thoughts by England given;
Her sights and sounds; dreams happy as her day;
    And laughter, learnt of friends; and gentleness,
        In hearts at peace, under an English heaven.

RUPERT BROOKE

gave, once, her flowers to love, her ways to roam...

the owl
looked up to the stars above,
and sang to a
small guitar...

The Owl and the Pussy-Cat

The Owl and the Pussy-Cat went to sea
In a beautiful pea-green boat,
They took some honey, and plenty of money,
Wrapped up in a five-pound note.
The Owl looked up to the stars above,
And sang to a small guitar,
'O lovely Pussy! O Pussy, my love,
What a beautiful Pussy you are,
You are,
You are!
What a beautiful Pussy you are!'

Pussy said to the Owl, 'You elegant fowl!
How charmingly sweet you sing!
O let us be married! too long we have tarried:
But what shall we do for a ring?'
They sailed away for a year and a day,
To the land where the Bong-tree grows,
And there in a wood a Piggy-wig stood,
With a ring at the end of his nose,
His nose,
His nose,
With a ring at the end of his nose.

'Dear Pig, are you willing to sell for one shilling
Your ring?' Said the Piggy, 'I will.'
So they took it away, and were married next day
By the Turkey who lives on the hill.
They dined on mince, and slices of quince,
Which they ate with a runcible spoon;
And hand in hand, on the edge of the sand,
They danced by the light of the moon,
The moon,
The moon,
They danced by the light of the moon.

EDWARD LEAR

Leisure

What is this life if, full of care,
We have no time to stand and stare.

No time to stand beneath the boughs
And stare as long as sheep or cows.

No time to see, when woods we pass,
Where squirrels hide their nuts in grass.

No time to see, in broad daylight,
Streams full of stars like skies at night.

No time to turn at Beauty's glance,
And watch her feet, how they can dance.

No time to wait till her mouth can
Enrich that smile her eyes began.

A poor life this if, full of care,
We have no time to stand and stare.

WILLIAM HENRY DAVIES

stand beneath
the boughs and stare
as long as sheep or cows...

for while the
tired waves,
vainly breaking...

Say Not the Struggle Nought Availeth

Say not the struggle nought availeth,
　　The labour and the wounds are vain,
The enemy faints not, nor faileth,
　　And as things have been, things remain.

If hopes were dupes, fears may be liars;
　　It may be, in yon smoke concealed,
Your comrades chase e'en now the fliers,
　　And, but for you, possess the field.

For while the tired waves, vainly breaking,
　　Seem here no painful inch to gain,
Far back through creeks and inlets making
　　Came, silent, flooding in, the main,

And not by eastern windows only,
　　When daylight comes, comes in the light,
In front the sun climbs slow, how slowly,
　　But westward, look, the land is bright.

ARTHUR HUGH CLOUGH

Solitude

Laugh, and the world laughs with you,
　　Weep, and you weep alone,
For sad old earth must borrow its mirth,
　　But has trouble enough of its own.
Sing, and the hills will answer;
　　Sigh, it is lost on the air,
The echoes bound to a joyful sound,
　　But shrink from voicing care.

Rejoice, and men will seek you;
　　Grieve, and they turn and go.
They want full measure of all your pleasure.
　　But they do not need your woe.
Be glad, and your friends are many,
　　Be sad, and you lose them all;
There are none to decline your nectared wine,
　　But alone you must drink life's gall.

Feast, and your halls are crowded,
　　Fast, and the world goes by.
Succeed and give – and it helps you live,
　　But no man can help you die;
There is room in the halls of pleasure
　　For a large and lordly train,
But one by one we must all file on
　　Through the narrow aisles of pain.

ELLA WHEELER WILCOX

sing, and the hills will answer...

On First Looking Into Chapman's Homer

Much have I travelled in the realms of gold,
  And many goodly states and kingdoms seen;
  Round many western islands have I been
Which bards in fealty to Apollo hold.
Oft of one wide expanse had I been told
  That deep-browed Homer ruled as his demesne:
  Yet did I never breathe its pure serene
Till I heard Chapman speak out loud and bold:
Then felt I like some watcher of the skies
  When a new planet swims into his ken;
Or like stout Cortez, when with eagle eyes
  He stared at the Pacific – and all his men
Looked at each other with a wild surmise –
  Silent, upon a peak in Darien.

JOHN KEATS

many goodly states and kingdoms seen...

my **heart** in him
his thoughts and **senses**
guides...

The Bargain

My true love hath my heart, and I have his,
      By just exchange, one for the other given.
I hold his dear, and mine he cannot miss,
      There never was a better bargain driven.
His heart in me keeps me and him in one,
      My heart in him his thoughts and senses guides;
He loves my heart, for once it was his own,
      I cherish his, because in me it bides.
His heart his wound receivèd from my sight,
      My heart was wounded with his wounded heart;
For as from me on him his hurt did light,
      So still methought in me his hurt did smart.
            Both equal hurt, in this change sought our bliss:
            My true love hath my heart and I have his.

SIR PHILIP SIDNEY

to bend with **apples** the **mossed** cottage-trees...

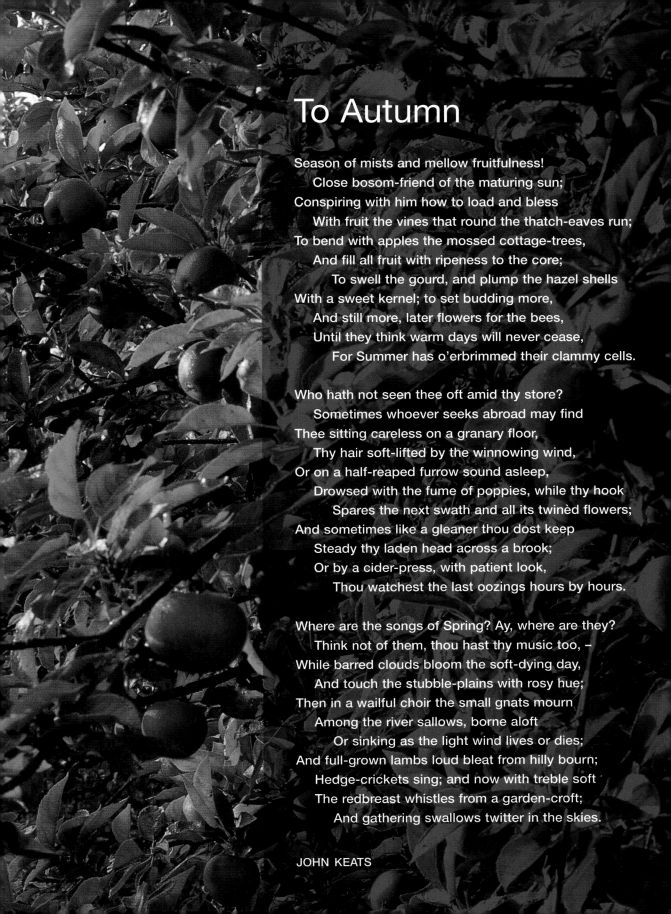

To Autumn

Season of mists and mellow fruitfulness!
   Close bosom-friend of the maturing sun;
Conspiring with him how to load and bless
   With fruit the vines that round the thatch-eaves run;
To bend with apples the mossed cottage-trees,
   And fill all fruit with ripeness to the core;
      To swell the gourd, and plump the hazel shells
With a sweet kernel; to set budding more,
   And still more, later flowers for the bees,
   Until they think warm days will never cease,
      For Summer has o'erbrimmed their clammy cells.

Who hath not seen thee oft amid thy store?
   Sometimes whoever seeks abroad may find
Thee sitting careless on a granary floor,
   Thy hair soft-lifted by the winnowing wind,
Or on a half-reaped furrow sound asleep,
   Drowsed with the fume of poppies, while thy hook
      Spares the next swath and all its twinèd flowers;
And sometimes like a gleaner thou dost keep
   Steady thy laden head across a brook;
   Or by a cider-press, with patient look,
      Thou watchest the last oozings hours by hours.

Where are the songs of Spring? Ay, where are they?
   Think not of them, thou hast thy music too, –
While barred clouds bloom the soft-dying day,
   And touch the stubble-plains with rosy hue;
Then in a wailful choir the small gnats mourn
   Among the river sallows, borne aloft
      Or sinking as the light wind lives or dies;
And full-grown lambs loud bleat from hilly bourn;
   Hedge-crickets sing; and now with treble soft
   The redbreast whistles from a garden-croft;
      And gathering swallows twitter in the skies.

JOHN KEATS

and **post** o'er
land and **ocean**
without **rest...**

On His Blindness

When I consider how my light is spent,

Ere half my days, in this dark world and wide,

And that one talent which is death to hide

Lodged with me useless, though my soul more bent

To serve therewith my Maker, and present

My true account, lest he returning chide,

'Doth God exact day-labour, light denied?'

I fondly ask. But Patience, to prevent

That murmur, soon replies: 'God doth not need

Either man's work or his own gifts; who best

Bear his mild yoke, they serve him best. His state

Is kingly: thousands at his bidding speed,

And post o'er land and ocean without rest;

They also serve who only stand and wait.'

JOHN MILTON

'How do I love thee? Let me count the ways'

How do I love thee? Let me count the ways.
I love thee to the depth and breadth and height
My soul can reach, when feeling out of sight
For the ends of Being and ideal Grace.
I love thee to the level of every day's
Most quiet need, by sun and candlelight.
I love thee freely, as men strive for Right;
I love thee purely, as they turn from Praise.
I love thee with the passion put to use
In my old griefs, and with my childhood's faith.
I love thee with a love I seemed to lose
With my lost saints, – I love thee with the breath,
Smiles, tears, of all my life! – and, if God choose,
I shall but love thee better after death.

ELIZABETH BARRETT BROWNING

I love thee to the
level of every day's
most quiet need...

the house
where I was born,
the little window...

I Remember,
I Remember

I remember, I remember,
The house where I was born,
The little window where the sun
Came peeping in at morn;
He never came a wink too soon,
Nor brought too long a day,
But now, I often wish the night
Had borne my breath away!

I remember, I remember,
The roses, red and white,
The violets, and the lily-cups,
Those flowers made of light!
The lilacs where the robin built,
And where my brother set
The laburnum on his birthday, –
The tree is living yet!

I remember, I remember,
Where I was used to swing,
And thought the air must rush as fresh
To swallows on the wing;
My spirit flew in feathers then,
That is so heavy now,
And summer pools could hardly cool
The fever on my brow!

I remember, I remember,
The fir trees dark and high;
I used to think their slender tops
Were close against the sky:
It was a childish ignorance,
But now 'tis little joy
To know I'm farther off from heaven
Than when I was a boy.

THOMAS HOOD

To Daffodils

Fair daffodils, we weep to see
　　You haste away so soon;
As yet the early-rising sun
　　Has not attained his noon.
　　　　Stay, stay
　　　Until the hasting day
　　　　　Has run
　　　But to the evensong;
And, having prayed together, we
　　　Will go with you along.

We have short time to stay as you,
　　We have as short a spring;
As quick a growth to meet decay,
　　As you, or anything.
　　　　We die
　　　As your hours do, and dry
　　　　　Away
　　　Like to the summer's rain;
Or as the pearls of morning's dew,
　　　Ne'er to be found again.

ROBERT HERRICK

we weep to see
you haste
away so soon...

Jerusalem

And did those feet in ancient time
Walk upon England's mountains green?
And was the holy Lamb of God
On England's pleasant pastures seen?

And did the Countenance Divine
Shine forth upon our clouded hills?
And was Jerusalem builded here
Among these dark Satanic Mills?

Bring me my Bow of burning gold!
Bring me my Arrows of desire!
Bring me my Spear! O clouds, unfold!
Bring me my Chariot of fire!

I will not cease from Mental Fight,
Nor shall my Sword sleep in my hand,
Till we have built Jerusalem
In England's green and pleasant land.

till we have built

jerusalem in england's
green and pleasant land

Weathers

This is the weather the cuckoo likes,
    And so do I;
When showers betumble the chestnut spikes,
    And nestlings fly;
And the little brown nightingale bills his best,
And they sit outside 'The Traveller's Rest',
And maids come forth sprig-muslin drest,
And citizens dream of the South and West,
    And so do I.

This is the weather the shepherd shuns,
    And so do I;
When beeches drip in browns and duns,
    And thresh, and ply;
And hill-hid tides throb, throe on throe,
And meadow rivulets overflow,
And drops on gate-bars hang in a row,
And rooks in families homeward go,
    And so do I.

THOMAS HARDY

this is the weather the cuckoo likes, and so do I...

from The Lady of Shalott

On either side the river lie
Long fields of barley and of rye,
That clothe the wold and meet the sky;
And through the field the road runs by
    To many-towered Camelot;
And up and down the people go,
Gazing where the lilies blow
Round an island there below,
    The island of Shalott.

Willows whiten, aspens quiver,
Little breezes dusk and shiver
Through the wave that runs for ever
By the island in the river
    Flowing down to Camelot.
Four gray walls, and four gray towers,
Overlook a space of flowers,
And the silent isle imbowers
    The Lady of Shalott.

By the margin, willow-veiled,
Slide the heavy barges trailed
By slow horses; and unhailed
The shallop flitteth silken-sailed
    Skimming down to Camelot:
But who hath seen her wave her hand?
Or at the casement seen her stand?
Or is she known in all the land,
    The Lady of Shalott?

Only reapers, reaping early
In among the bearded barley,
Hear a song that echoes cheerly,
From the river winding clearly,
    Down to towered Camelot:
And by the moon the reaper weary,
Piling sheaves in uplands airy,
Listening, whispers ''Tis the fairy
    Lady of Shalott.'

ALFRED, LORD TENNYSON

the river winding clearly, down to towered camelot...

The Tiger

Tiger! Tiger! burning bright
In the forests of the night,
What immortal hand or eye
Could frame thy fearful symmetry?

In what distant deeps or skies
Burned the fire of thine eyes?
On what wings dare he aspire?
What the hand dare seize the fire?

tiger! tiger!

burning bright

in the forests of the night...

And what shoulder, and what art,

Could twist the sinews of thy heart?

And when thy heart began to beat,

What dread hand? And what dread feet?

What the hammer? What the chain?

In what furnace was thy brain?

What the anvil? What dread grasp

Dare its deadly terrors clasp?

When the stars threw down their spears,

And watered heaven with their tears,

Did he smile his work to see?

Did he who made the Lamb make thee?

Tiger! Tiger! burning bright

In the forests of the night,

What immortal hand or eye

Dare frame thy fearful symmetry?

WILLIAM BLAKE

the poppies blow
between the crosses,
row on row...

In Flanders Fields

In Flanders fields the poppies blow
Between the crosses, row on row,
    That mark our place; and in the sky
    The larks, still bravely singing, fly
Scarce heard amid the guns below.

We are the Dead. Short days ago
We lived, felt dawn, saw sunset glow,
    Loved and were loved, and now we lie
    In Flanders fields.

Take up our quarrel with the foe:
To you from failing hands we throw
    The torch; be yours to hold it high.
    If ye break faith with us who die
We shall not sleep, though poppies grow
    In Flanders fields.

JOHN McCRAE

from Ode to a Skylark

Hail to thee, blithe spirit!
Bird thou never wert –
That from heaven or near it
Pourest thy full heart
In profuse strains of unpremeditated art.

Higher still and higher
From the earth thou springest,
Like a cloud of fire;
The blue deep thou wingest,
And singing still dost soar, and soaring ever singest.

In the golden lightning
Of the sunken sun,
O'er which clouds are brightening,
Thou dost float and run,
Like an unbodied joy whose race is just begun.

The pale purple even
Melts around thy flight;
Like a star of heaven,
In the broad daylight
Thou art unseen, but yet I hear thy shrill delight –

PERCY BYSSHE SHELLEY

and singing still dost soar, and soaring ever singest...

at the foot of thy crags, o sea!

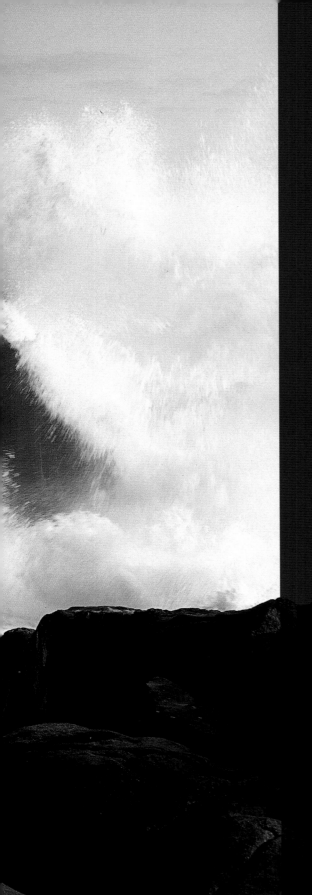

Break, Break, Break

Break, break, break,
      On thy cold gray stones, O Sea!
And I would that my tongue could utter
      The thoughts that arise in me.

O well for the fisherman's boy,
      That he shouts with his sister at play!
O well for the sailor lad,
      That he sings in his boat on the bay!

And the stately ships go on
      To their haven under the hill;
But O for the touch of a vanished hand,
      And the sound of a voice that is still!

Break, break, break,
      At the foot of thy crags, O Sea!
But the tender grace of a day that is dead
      Will never come back to me.

ALFRED, LORD TENNYSON

if you can **wait** and not be tired by **waiting…**

If

If you can keep your head when all about you
    Are losing theirs and blaming it on you;
If you can trust yourself when all men doubt you,
    But make allowance for their doubting too;
If you can wait and not be tired by waiting,
    Or being lied about, don't deal in lies,
Or being hated, don't give way to hating,
    And yet don't look too good, nor talk too wise:

If you can dream – and not make dreams your master;
    If you can think – and not make thoughts your aim;
If you can meet with Triumph and Disaster
    And treat those two impostors just the same;
If you can bear to hear the truth you've spoken
    Twisted by knaves to make a trap for fools,
Or watch the things you gave your life to, broken,
    And stoop and build 'em up with worn-out tools:

If you can make one heap of all your winnings
    And risk it on one turn of pitch-and-toss,
And lose, and start again at your beginnings
    And never breathe a word about your loss;
If you can force your heart and nerve and sinew
    To serve your turn long after they are gone,
And so hold on when there is nothing in you
    Except the Will which says to them: 'Hold on!'

If you can talk with crowds and keep your virtue,
    Or walk with Kings – nor lose the common touch,
If neither foes nor loving friends can hurt you,
    If all men count with you, but none too much;
If you can fill the unforgiving minute
    With sixty seconds' worth of distance run,
Yours is the Earth and everything that's in it,
    And – which is more – you'll be a Man, my son!

RUDYARD KIPLING.

Loveliest of Trees

Loveliest of trees, the cherry now
Is hung with bloom along the bough,
And stands about the woodland ride
Wearing white for Eastertide.

Now, of my threescore years and ten,
Twenty will not come again,
And take from seventy springs a score,
It only leaves me fifty more.

And since to look at things in bloom
Fifty springs are little room,
About the woodlands I will go
To see the cherry hung with snow.

ALFRED EDWARD HOUSMAN

the cherry now
is hung with
bloom along the bough...

England

No lovelier hills than thine have laid
   My tired thoughts to rest;
No peace of lovelier valleys made
   Like peace within my breast.

Thine are the woods whereto my soul,
   Out of the noontide beam,
Flees for a refuge green and cool
   And tranquil as a dream.

Thy breaking seas like trumpets peal;
   Thy clouds – how oft have I
Watched their bright towers of silence steal
   Into infinity!

My heart within me faints to roam
   In thought even far from thee:
Thine be the grave whereto I come,
   And thine my darkness be.

WALTER DE LA MARE

no lovelier hills
than thine have laid...

The Donkey

When fishes flew and forests walked
    And figs grew upon thorn,
Some moment when the moon was blood
    Then surely I was born;

With monstrous head and sickening cry
    And ears like errant wings,
The devil's walking parody
    On all four-footed things.

The tattered outlaw of the earth,
    Of ancient crooked will;
Starve, scourge, deride me: I am dumb,
    I keep my secret still.

Fools! For I also had my hour;
    One far fierce hour and sweet:
There was a shout about my ears,
    And palms before my feet.

GILBERT KEITH CHESTERTON

with **monstrous** **head** and sickening cry and ears like **errant** wings...

with a cargo
of ivory, and
apes and peacocks…

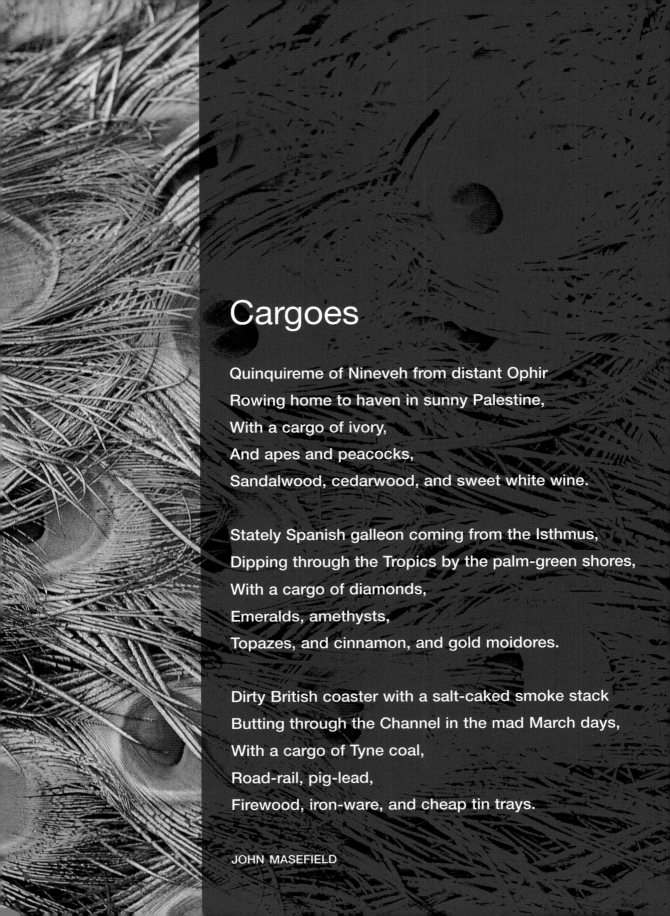

Cargoes

Quinquireme of Nineveh from distant Ophir
Rowing home to haven in sunny Palestine,
With a cargo of ivory,
And apes and peacocks,
Sandalwood, cedarwood, and sweet white wine.

Stately Spanish galleon coming from the Isthmus,
Dipping through the Tropics by the palm-green shores,
With a cargo of diamonds,
Emeralds, amethysts,
Topazes, and cinnamon, and gold moidores.

Dirty British coaster with a salt-caked smoke stack
Butting through the Channel in the mad March days,
With a cargo of Tyne coal,
Road-rail, pig-lead,
Firewood, iron-ware, and cheap tin trays.

JOHN MASEFIELD

from The Old Ships

I have seen old ships sail like swans asleep
Beyond the village which men still call Tyre,
With leaden age o'ercargoed, dipping deep
For Famagusta and the hidden sun
That rings black Cyprus with a lake of fire;
And all those ships were certainly so old,
Who knows how oft with squat and noisy gun,
Questing brown slaves or Syrian oranges,
The pirates Genoese
Hell-raked them till they rolled
Blood, water, fruit and corpses up the hold.
But now through friendly seas they softly run,
Painted the mid-sea blue or shore-sea green,
Still patterned with the vine and grapes in gold.

JAMES ELROY FLECKER

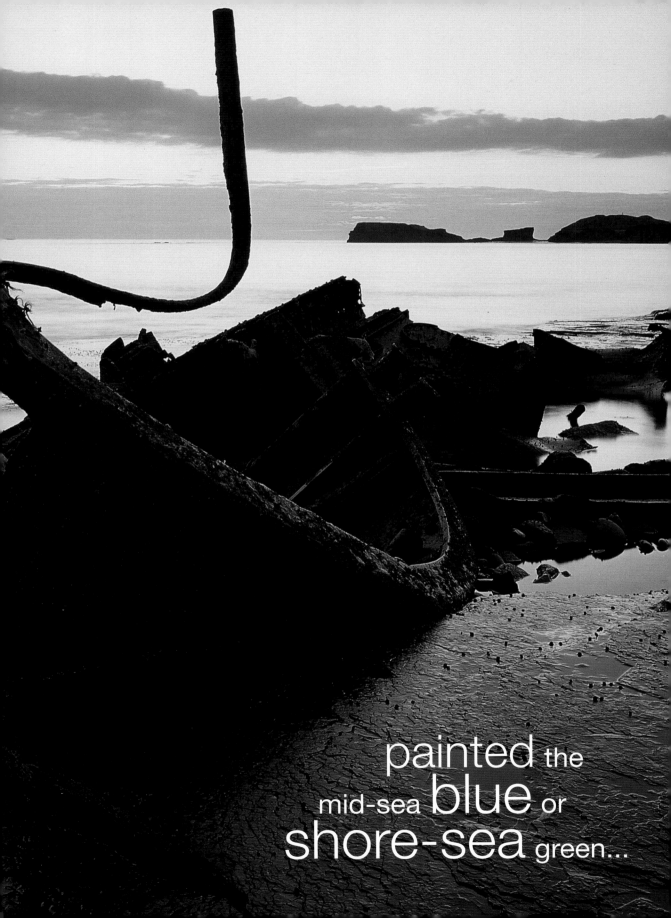

painted the
mid-sea blue or
shore-sea green...

When You Are Old

When you are old and grey and full of sleep,
   And, nodding by the fire, take down this book,
   And slowly read, and dream of the soft look
Your eyes had once, and of their shadows deep;

How many loved your moments of glad grace,
   And loved your beauty with love false or true;
   But one man loved the pilgrim soul in you,
And loved the sorrows of your changing face.

And bending down beside the glowing bars,
   Murmur, a little sadly, how love fled
   And paced upon the mountains overhead,
And hid his face amid a crowd of stars.

WILLIAM BUTLER YEATS

nodding by
the fire, take
down this book...

ACKNOWLEDGEMENTS

All the photographs in this book are all from the National Trust Picture Library
with the exception those of pages 74, 78 & 88 are reproduced courtesy of Ardea, London
and those on pages 10, 19 & 23 which are reproduced courtesy of The Travel Library.
Copyright is with the following photographers.

Ian Shaw p 59, 82; Ian West p 6, 22; John Blake p 8, 9; Travel Library p 10;
Stephen Robson p 12,14, 60; Nick Meers p 16, 30, 34, 38, 40; David Noton p 16, 20, 24, 29;
Derek Croucher p 18, 36, 58, 66; Philip Enticknap p 19; Lee Frost p 23; Dietmar Nill/Nature PL p 26;
Joe Cornish p 1, 2, 28, 46, 56, 80, 86, 92; David Sellman p 32, 63, 64; Michael Allwood-Coppin p 42;
D Kjaer p 44, 70; John Darley p 48; Simon King /Nature PL p 50; Dennis Davis p 52;
Jenny McMillan p 54; F Kersting p 62; Derry Robinson p 68, 76; Oliver Benn p 72;
Masahiro Iljima p 74; Derek Harris p 84; Ardea p 88; Neil Campbell-Sharp p 90; Simon Upton p 94

Cover image: Sheffield Park Gardens courtesy of the National Trust Picture Library/Stephen Robson.

Mr K. P. Griffin, on behalf of the Trustees of the Estate
of Mrs H. M. Davies, for 'Leisure' by W. H. Davies

The Society of Authors as the Literary Representative of the Estate of A. E. Housman,
for 'Loveliest of Trees' from A Shropshire Lad by A. E. Housman

A. P. Watt Ltd on behalf of The National Trust for Places of Historic Interest
or Natural Beauty for, 'If' by Rudyard Kipling, from The Definitive Edition
of Rudyard Kipling's Verse (Hodder and Stoughton 1940)

The Literary Trustees of Walter de la Mare and the Society of Authors
as their representative, for 'England' and 'Silver' by Walter de la Mare

The Society of Authors as the Literary Representative of the Estate
of John Masefield, for 'Sea-Fever' and 'Cargoes' by John Masefield

A. P. Watt Ltd on behalf of the Royal Literary Fund, for 'The Donkey' by G. K. Chesterton,
from The Collected Poems of G. K. Chesterton (Methuen & Co Ltd 1933).

A. P. Watt Ltd., Michael B. Yeats and Macmillan London Ltd., for 'The Lake Isle of Innisfree'
and 'When You Are Old', from The Collected Poems of W. B. Yeats

Every effort has been made to contact copyright holders.
We apologize for any unintentional errors or omissions.